The Girls of Peculiar

Catherine Pierce

saturnalia books

Distributed by University Press of New England
Hanover and London

The Girls of Peculiar

Saturnalia Books
105 Woodside Rd.
Ardmore, PA 19003
info@saturnaliabooks.com

ISBN: 978-0-9833686-2-5
Library of Congress Control Number: 2011945980

Book Design by Saturnalia Books
Printing by Westcan Printing Group, Canada

Cover Art: Matt Haber, *Delicate Rescue,* 2010
Photo credit: Megan Bean

Distributed by:
University Press of New England
1 Court Street
Lebanon, NH 03766
800-421-1561

Grateful acknowledgment is made to the publications where these poems first appeared, sometimes in different form.

AGNI online: "Firefly"
Anti-: "She Considers Trading Her Secrets," "Somewhere in the heap of minutes"
Bellingham Review: "Everything an Amulet or Omen," "Lamp," "Virginity"
Blackbird: "The Delinquent Girls," "The Quiet Girls," "The Drama Girls," "The Geek Girls," "She Gets Drunk and Talks Too Much at Her 20th Reunion"
Boston Review: "Dear Day"
The Cincinnati Review: "Dear Self I Might Have Been"
Copper Nickel: "Oregon Trail, 5th Grade," "The Sleeping Creature House"
Court Green: "Postcards from Her Alternate Lives," "The women from the '70s are beautiful"
Crab Orchard Review: "Reading YM at the Pool, Age 12," "The Guidance Counselor to the Girl"
diode: "How It Ends: Three Cities," "Train Safety Assembly," "The '70s Aren't Coming Back," "Scale," "For This You Have No Reason," "Because I'll Never Swim in Every Ocean"
FIELD: "Fire Blight," "The Universe is a Madam," "Without Ceremony"
Indiana Review: "Dear Atom Bomb," "Emergence"
Mid-American Review: "A Catalogue of My Wants from Age 16 to the Present"
New Madrid: "High School: A Triptych," "Maryland, 1964," "Postcards from Her Future Self"
Ninth Letter: "Pennsylvania, 1961"

The Paris Review Daily: "Hare-Lip"
Ploughshares: "A Short Biography of the American People by City," "The Books Fill Her Apartment Like Birds"
Slate: "Reading Faulkner at 17, You Foresee Your Reckoning"
Sixth Finch: "Poem to the Girls We Were," "Poem from the Girls We Were"
Superstition Review: "Narrative Theory"

"Postcards from Her Alternate Lives" also appears in *The Best American Poetry 2011*, edited by Kevin Young.

I am grateful for a grant from the Mississippi Arts Commission that helped support the writing of this book.

My sincere and serious thanks to the people who have helped to shape this book and the poems in it, in particular Brian Barker, Nicky Beer, Steve Gehrke, Becky Hagenston, Richard Lyons, Michael Kardos, and Maggie Smith. Thank you to Henry Israeli at Saturnalia Books. Thanks to my colleagues at Mississippi State University. Enormous thanks to my parents and sister for their unwavering support of what I do. And thank you, thank you, to Mike and to Sam, who fill every day with light.

for my family

TABLE OF CONTENTS

3.

1.

POEM TO THE GIRLS WE WERE

Give us back that simple guilt,
that red ache that came from lying
to our mothers. Look at you,
luxuriating in the bathwater of shame.
It's lovely, isn't it, to pity yourself
your unconscionable choices, to look
in the mirror at your doe eyes,
your mouths ripe and pitiably slack?
Listen. Give us back the rumor
whispers if you can't appreciate them.
Yes, we recall how the hot throb
radiated, like a jellyfish binding
our organs in its poison strands,
but it's now now, and from here
that throb is simply the sun on a too-
bright day. And you're the one
choosing to stay outside. Give us back
our fears. You doze inside them,
wrap yourselves in them like sable.
Yes, they're plush, and The Future
is a century away, and you know
your legs are transcendent, you know,
as we did, how to tug each grief-gilded
string to make the world dance any way
your gorgeous, guilty selves want.

THE DELINQUENT GIRLS

Were we never stones? No, we never were.
The day never washed over us. We never cooled
with twilight. We were busy prowling

by the river, sending our lit eyes into tree hollows,
beneath parked cars. We kept our muscles taut
with running. We outpaced each other. Our hackles

up all night, the wind an accomplice, or sometimes
a snitch. When the sun came up, we were near dead,
smiling in our sleep, our big teeth showing. When

the dark rolled round again, we were silver-sighted,
wrapped in smoke and ready. We howled. Oh yes.
Listen. Our throats still know how to find the rawest song.

Oregon Trail, 5th Grade

"You may: 1. Travel the trail. 2. Learn about the trail. 3. See the Oregon Top Ten. 4. Turn sound off. 5. Choose Management Options. 6. End. What is your choice?"

—opening screen of the Oregon Trail computer game

First, choose your name. Pluck the letters,
roll them in your mouth—finally the swirls of the S
and the Ls, not the rough cough of the K.
Now, choose your life. Bankers have everything,
but there's no reward in ease. Farmers die
early, and the point is survival. So choose
the middle, you're no fool. Carpenters are dull,
but they can do. Like you. The other kids
are idiots, loading up on clothes and corn,
but you know the trick: ammo, oxen, and luck.
The kids are squirrelish, chattery. They poke
and giggle. Meanwhile, you're gone.

You're wagon master, with your S and your Ls,
and you're going to school the West. You'll manifest
your own destiny and devil take the doubters
(you learned the phrase in a snuck book
and for days you've hoarded it). You know each pixel
of the screen's hot blues and greens, each flat,
bold note that sounds when someone succumbs
to typhoid. You fill out the grave, guiltless, gleeful:
Here lies Clara, a proper fool. Typhoid sounds to you
like a windstorm, like dumb Clara died when her heart
thrashed too hard against the limbs of her ribs.

You glance around the room. Kids snickering,
scratching notes, no one serious. Fools
and doubters, dumb Claras all. You pray typhoid
for all of them. Let them see what it's like to feel
their insides lash and shudder. Let them know
what you know. Meanwhile, you level your rifle.
Meanwhile, you ford the river. The whole
green country is yours. You're almost there.

Dear Atom Bomb,

I confess—you were my high school obsession.
You bloomed inside my chest until I howled. You shook me
with your booming zillion wattage. You were bigger
than rock and roll. I lost days to you, the way you expanded

to become more than even yourself. In Science class
movies, you puffed men like microwaved marshmallows,
raked blood from their insides, and always I could feel
your heat like a massive cloak around my shoulders.

You embarrassed me. You were too depraved for dignity,
not caring whose eyes you melted, whose innards oozed;
you balled up control in your God-huge palms
and tossed it into the stratosphere. Oh, Atom Bomb,

I miss you. These days my mind is no incandescent
blur but a narrow infrared beam spotlighting
bounded fears: cancer in a single throat; a shock
of blood on the clean sheets; a careless turn from

the grocery store lot into the pickup with the pit bull
in the bed. Oh, Atom Bomb, come back. Take me away
from the twitch in my leg, the cracking lead paint,
the lurking salmonella. Sweep me up in your blinding

white certainty. Make me sure once again that
I'll live till the world's brilliant end.

THE QUIET GIRLS

Were we never wolves? No, we never were.
We never let ourselves be lured into a lair.
We never licked honey off an eyetooth

just for the sweet. We never swallowed
our own blood with the honey. We were
neither animal nor stone. We were ephemeral,

motes in light, breath in winter. Drifting
was safe travel; we knew it then, and we were right.
The earth slowed its spinning and we stayed on.

Trenches yawned, and we skirted them. We survived
the meteor shower—no fragments fell on us.
Still we float like spores, always aloft and away.

THE CHILD HAS READ EVERYTHING

And everything is haunted: the storybook where girls
in dirndls are devoured. Her mother's silver-spined
paperbacks that heat her in dark places. The newspaper
with its front page bloodied by the car crash. She can't

stop her eyes. She tries to forget what she's read, but
like that other story, once she's bitten in, she can't untaste.
Her mind won't listen, veers off into the forest marked

Forbidden, holds a knife to her throat when she begs it
to stop. For safety, she drinks her own guilt. It inoculates her.
Everyone thinks she is the good daughter,
her world a gold-leaf illustration. No one knows

the words seed themselves in her brain. That they grow
and grow, their roots tangled, their limbs goblin-fingered.
No one hears how they whisper, *Think me.* The words

blacken and climb until she can't see past their spiny tops.
Even as the world goes on real around her, she is shadowed.
Sometimes light flickers above the clawed trees, and in it
she can make out people moving. They laugh like the dragon

isn't always behind them. Like the limbs aren't full
of hanged children, swinging. Like they have never
watched, horrified, their minds race over the landscape

like escaped hounds. She aches toward the people. But then
the pages open again and she gorges herself to sickness.
She doesn't want to find the path. She's the wicked daughter,
the one who stays lost, and she'll learn that story by heart.

She'll dwell in her own darkness, grow lizard-lidded,
cat-limbed. She'll drink her evil down. She'll twist the trees
into every shape but the one that reads The End.

NARRATIVE THEORY

I was in Italy once and there was a mask shop.
I was in Italy once and there was a bridge.

I was twenty and wandering the country
like I wandered my mind. The sweat-and-cigarette-
packed metro, the stains on the hostel pillow,

even the knife-eyed men calling across alleys
came through in soft focus. I filed them away, all under S

for Story. I was in Italy once, and I was sick,
as sick as I've ever been. My throat swelled
and my chest filled with pebbles. My heart clattered

like a roughshod horse if I walked up a flight
of steps. But I ate cheese and bread heartily,

thinking, like Heidi, it would make me strong.
It didn't, but days went by and I forgot, slowly,
the frantic thumping. I was in Italy once and I drank

cooking sherry from a jug. Someone laughed, and I
filed that away, too. I was in Italy once, on a payphone

on a dock on an island. A man approached, and I spoke
the language brokenly, said "phone" and "United
States" and he nodded and stepped back. It was,

inexplicably, my proudest moment. I was in Italy
once and I watched a curtain of pigeons lift

over St. Mark's Square. I thought, *I am watching this.*
I thought, *what a good word: curtain.* Later,
I ate tiramisu on the canal and was aware

of doing so. I was always aware of doing so.
In Venice I thought the clouds were mountains

in the distance, and made a note of my foolishness.
Later, I realized they were. I was in Italy once
and thought I could tell my own story.

SHE GETS DRUNK AND TALKS TOO MUCH
AT HER 20TH REUNION

Used to be I was locked in the future. And the future
was no blank canvas, was no white page, but
was crammed with graveyards and rivers and red-eyes.
All black and green and gold, all sailing-off-the-edge,
all how-do-you-know-which-mushrooms-are-poison?
Used to be everyone said *baby* in my fantasies,
but mainly my fantasies were silent, occasional voices
flapping past the moving windows, aural hitchhikers.
Used to be I'd pick the voices up for a while, then
drop them in the next town. If they got rough, the gun
came out. Used to be I was going to ride horses and sail
schooners. I was always going to have twelve babies,
and they were all going to live. Sometimes the future
was the prairie in 1870. I wore hay in my hair
and howled till the wind matched my pitch. Sometimes
it was Fenwick Island in the '60s, and I saved
men and children from the snarling waves. Sometimes
I crawled through movie screens and snatched plastic
apples right from the almost-bite of starlets. The starlets
hated me. Because I could climb out of the screen again.
They wanted to leave. *Oh, baby,* I told the girls, *everybody*
wants to leave. It's when you stop wanting it you're in trouble.

THE GEEK GIRLS

Were we never robins? No, we never were.
No one recognized spring in us, though great elms
grew inside our rib cages. They pushed their spiny

tips outward, so that we felt small stabbings daily,
but they never broke through. So we were never spring,
never foliage. We were the small and oddball beasts:

anoles, silverfish, shrimp. We moved fast and sideways,
upways, allways but straight. We heard of nights lit
with lightning bugs and cigarettes. With rumflame

and tonguefire. We needed none of it. The nights were
black puzzleboxes and we solved them. It was easy then—
in the darkness, our minds sparked like flint.

FIREFLY

Its six legs coated with disease, it's vulgar
like the aphid, the earwig. Its eyes are nightmare

globes. It does not love you or thank you
for the glass jar with air holes. Still, you want it

in your hands. Not for its yellow light like the soft
glow in the wooded cabin. Not for the vibrating

wings against your palms like champagne
bubbles bursting. Not even for the perfect

metaphors that ride on its sunflower-seed back—
the catching of a gone childhood, the art

of keeping something alive. You pursue it
because it's a slow beast, easily captured. Because

it hovers and floats. Because you can win at this,
and because it will fly off when you unfold

your hands, single-minded, unmoved by its loss.

Dear Self I Might Have Been,

Did you ever make it to Taos, the Badlands, the Isle
of Skye, all the places you thought you'd locate yourself,

as if you might have been hiding in a whisky cask
or buried by earthquake rubble? I suspect, Self

I Might Have Been, that you didn't. I suspect
that you spent the long highway days of your twenties

surrounded by photographs and harmonica songs, the future
a galaxy hurtling above you, infinite and too far

to touch, and your body always alive with nerves and hope,
your hunger for Next pushing that other hunger

to the side until you became thin as a plunging star's trail,
your eyes larger and larger until they could take in

all the sky's dome at once. And I suspect that you loved
so much this launch phase—the roar, the flames, the fear—

that the cubicle at your filing job, the elm-lined streets
of your hometown became lit with a heat

stronger than the desert, with vistas more awful
than the Badlands, with desolation greater and greener

than that Scottish isle, and once you saw your world
in its true vastness, you knew you'd never leave it.

TRAIN SAFETY ASSEMBLY

Each spring, they made us watch
the movie: kids in their striped '70s shirts,
foolish on the tracks, all gumption
and bravado, all *we'll-be-back-in-time-*
for-dinner, then the laces wrapped
on a spike, a scream, a cut to white.
I carried the movie like a door
behind my ribs. Sometimes
it swung into a starless black.

Once, my cousin placed a penny
on the tracks behind her house as I
hissed and moaned from the back door.
The next day, she pressed the flat
President into my palm. The copper
burned with her narrow escape.
Keep it, she said. *I'll do it again.*

A train is no mind, no give, just
roar and edge. What kept me up
was how it didn't care for me.
How its churning covered no mercy.
How its bright, unlidded eye
cut right through fog.

I would like to end with an idea
of, say, travel: that fear of trains is fear
of leaving, or that the metal bellow
is the sound of swift distance. But
it would be a lie. The train is simply
the opposite of what I want my life to be.
On the other hand, it never flinches.

THE DRAMA GIRLS

Were we never a still lake? No, we never were.
We never reflected back anything but ourselves.
We never shifted subtle with the wind. It was not

our desire. We were our desire. We were bird
cries, sudden and more obscene than was necessary.
We were paste jewels glinting in pines. We were

never the lake, but we were the lakeside creatures,
soft-bellied, begging. We rolled over to be patted,
and then we put teeth to skin. And then we rolled

again. These days ache. We send our voices out
into air, and air eats them. We are meant to be thrown
stones. Where is the mirrored sky for us to shatter?

POEM FROM THE GIRLS WE WERE

You're kidding, right? You want
this back? This all-night nausea,
this skull-splitting what-is-it?
You want, again, to sit quaking
in a rusted Dodge, afraid of your own
rage firefighting inside you? That heat
you recall is no sun, and no jellyfish, either—
it's a planet exploding with you
at its molten center. Come sit amidst
these songs again and tell us you want
to live here. The churning organ
digs a hole and we crawl dutifully
inside. We apply the rasping voices
like a poultice. Trust us: this is
no romance. This is flames
in the fingers and a frozen gullet.
This is every house on your block
lit from within, each bedroom window
shining with safety and you outside
in the icing dusk, knowing nothing
will ever warm you. This is the gray
song you'll hear forever. Your bones
will stay marrowed with dust.
The Future? This is The Future.
If you were here, you'd know that.

2.

Because I'll Never Swim in Every Ocean

Want is ten thousand blue feathers falling
all around me, and me unable to stomach
that I might catch five but never ten thousand.
So I drop my hands to my sides and wait
to be buried. I open a book and the words
spring and taunt. Flashes—*motel, lapidary,*
piranha—of every story, every poem I'll never
know well enough to conjure in sleep.
What's the point of words if I can't
own them all? I toss book after book
into my imaginary trashcan fire.
Or I think I'll learn piano. At the first lesson,
we're clapping whole and half notes
and this is childish, I'm better than this.
I'd like to leave playing Ravel. I'd like
to give a concerto on Saturday. So I quit.
I have standards. Then on Saturday,
I have a beer, watch a telethon. Or
we watch a documentary on Antarctica.
The interviewees are from Belarus, Lima, Berlin.
Everyone speaks English. Everyone names
a philosopher, an ethos. One man carries a raft
on his back at all times. I went to Nebraska once
and swore it was a great adventure. It was.
I think of how I'll never go to Antarctica,
mainly because I don't much want to. But
I should want to. I should be the girl

with a raft on her back. When I think
of all the mountains and monuments
and skyscapes I haven't seen, all the trains
I should take, all the camels and mopeds
and ferries I should ride, all the scorching
hikes I should nearly die on, I press
my body down, down into the vast green
couch. If I step out the door, the infinity
of what I've missed will zorro me across
the face with a big L for *Lazy*. Sometimes
I watch finches at the feeder, their bodies small
suns, and have to grab the sill to steady myself.
Metaphorically, of course. I'm no loon.
Look—even my awestruck is half-assed.
But I'm so tired of the small steps—
the pentatonic scale, the frequent flyer
hoarding, the one exquisite sentence
in a forest of exquisite sentences.
There is a globe welling up inside of me.
Mountain ranges ridging my skin,
oceans filling my mouth. If I stay still
long enough, I could become my own world.

FIRE BLIGHT

Def: A plant disease that has destroyed pear and apple orchards in much of North America, parts of Europe, New Zealand, and Japan...Pears, apples, crab apples, and quinces appear as if scorched by fire.

—*Encyclopedia Britannica*

You're sixteen. You carry a camera—a real one,
you're learning words like *aperture* and *F-stop*.
You're sixteen. You've stopped brushing your hair,
and would like someone to ask why you've stopped
brushing your hair. You're thinking of dyeing
the tangles plum. You're thinking of. You're sixteen.

Last year you weighed more. This year you're as tall
as you'll get, and there's a boy whose eyes are poisoned
marbles. You've photographed him again and again
but you can't get the poison right. You're sixteen.
You say this again and again but you can't believe it.
In Bio, your friend shows you her bruised stomach.

We didn't use a condom, she whispers, *so I was careful.*
You blink. Down the rabbit hole. Your teacher
drones about splitting the atom and you imagine
your imperfect young skin melting and feel a tenderness
for yourself that surprises you. Slides of destruction
flash on the cinderblock wall. A girl missing her face.

A fetus in a jar. An entire orchard stripped and blackened.
Once, your grandfather's apple tree had sickened and died.
The grass littered with apples, shining brown and wrongly.
A fairytale curse, you'd thought. You think it now.
The poison-eyed boy ruins everything with words.
He wants you to be a dropped fruit, a twisted vine.

But you're not ill. You're not twisted. You're sixteen.
You're fire-clean. You're purified. You know when
to shut up and look. Who could snap the shutter
on the missing-face girl? Who could stand
in the half-light of the floating fetus and document?
Someone impervious. Someone already in flames.

THE UNIVERSE IS A MADAM

Your star-marked hair is set
with laissez-faire,
but you blink and comets
hightail it. All my life I've tried
to be like you. All my life
I've failed. What do I have to do
to match your husk-voice, your red-
light-pulse? You with your
Spin inside me, worlds. Your
Today a fire appears, today one blackens.
Some nights I walk through
my silent neighborhood with my head down.
I'm giving you a chance, Universe.
Pluck me up. Scold me. Tell me
I'm failing, that the clients
have complained. Then give me
one more chance. *Go,* I'd like to
hear you say, supernovas churning
inside your gaping mouth,
and make me proud.

When Things Are Going Poorly, Places I Would Rather Be:

The circus, nineteen rows back, far enough that if
      the tiger escapes, it will eat everyone else first.

Underwater, listening to the tiny mouths of fish
      as they crunch delicate coral. But breathing. This is important.

In the outer space dream I once had. Me, floating,
      surrounded by dark and palm-sized stars. And not alone.

Suspended in the ruby glow of just-too-much tempranillo,
      which is to say, just enough.

Above the tree line, steeped in pine and air thin as sun glints,
      unable to draw the right breath and fixated, for now, on that.

READING FAULKNER AT 17,
YOU FORESEE YOUR RECKONING

The harvest moon hangs heavy,
a gourd. Your desires heave inside you
like a blood wave. Ignore the cat

pulling on your trousers. Ignore
the cicadas bossing you from the elms.
See yourself in this hot gold light.

You are the brother in love with Caddy.
You are the idiot son. Your mouth dumb.
Your mind lucent. Everything you want

sharp as the cat's bite at your ankle. You pull
your foot back. A yowl, pointed as teeth.
The moon is what will fall on you.

THE WOMEN FROM THE '70S ARE BEAUTIFUL

in photographs, their eyes always wheel-large and dark,
rimmed with charcoal in the way no one does anymore except
embarrassed and angry 10th graders but in photographs
the women from the '70s don't look embarrassed,

unless it's in a slight, elfin way that makes you think of cocaine
lines and white lies, and anyway, most of them look
instead like deer, like aspen, like anything too leggy and proud

to ride in lumbering Chevys but unafraid in their height and angles
and always the huge dark eyes, the hair somehow long and big at once
and draped like sealskin over their shoulders, and the women

are always laughing toward something out of frame,
a mirror ball or a Ferris wheel or the boy they someday divorced
and what is most beautiful is how they are always looking
away, how very much they don't need you at all.

Postcards from Her Future Self

1.
Trust me when I tell you to take that trip to Aspen.

2.
You will find yourself in an aviary. Though you hate the birds' gray
spindle legs, hold yourself together. Wait until the kestrel looks at you.
That moment will allow you the flying dreams you long for.

3.
The man in the awful orange tie? Notice his right eye. When it twitches
he is about to shriek like a caught cat. Leave the Indian restaurant before
this happens. Otherwise, you will see him down dark alleys for years.
Though if you stick around, the waitress will bring a free lassi.

4.
600 thread count sheets are worth it. Though you cringe now, someday
you'll think so. Don't leave the full cart in the middle of the aisle.
It isn't the act of liberation you believe it to be.

5.
Your first haircut after your divorce will be disastrous.

6.
Unless you learn to love the railroad watch he gives you. Unless
you come to choose Cooperstown over Glens Falls. Unless you stop
worrying the Bananas Foster will rot your molars. In which case
there will be no disastrous haircut.

7.

Remember Rocco, the small white dog of your adolescence. This is not
a question, but an imperative. Remember him. His yapping deafness.
His matted mutt fur. You loved him, though not deeply. Once,
you walked him at dusk and he barked at a mailbox. Take care
to remember your least important days with fondness.

Virginity

"Chastity was in former times considered a girl's most prized treasure, reflected in the special magical status accorded to virgins in many cultures."

—*Cassell's Dictionary of Superstitions*

Baby, I said no. Of course I feel it, too.
Of course that Hammond organ vibrating fatly
through the speakers is almost enough to spring
the mouse trap of my body. Your hand on my neck
is electroshock therapy and I'm nearly cured.

But if I give in, who will save me from the killer bees?
Now I can sing inside their tornado, unstung. I can
lean back in the chaise and watch the sun float across
the sky all day like a double-feature on repeat—
no phantoms fogging my eyes, just light, light, light.

You can snap a candle out, but I can snap it back
to flame. Darling, I'm bell-jarred, but it's all for you.
What happens when the swarm surrounds us, when
a blackout blinds the city, when a unicorn bolts across
Hudson? Only I can coax the world back into place.

You say the city is concrete and wire and nothing
else. You say there is no unicorn, and the sun
will sear anyone who stares. You say *Hush, honey.*
You say *Lie back, just listen.* But, baby, I am
listening. All I hear is how much you need me.

HIGH SCHOOL: A TRIPTYCH

I. How Each Day Goes

Limbed like a frozen willow, all night she crawls through
dreams. In them, clouds gather. Then vast, screaming squalls through

placid skies. At dawn she rises, healthy with rage. In chorus
she inks stars on her arms. Her voice—sand, shards—stalls through

its mincing solo. Girls pass looks above her hair. Its knots
are artful plums. Awkward boys love her. She enthralls through

her angles, her laugh like a cough. She smokes for the Zippo
flick. Her eyes, bird-quick, are elsewhere. All through

Mr. Steele's New Deal lecture, she sketches snow banks,
imagines the flakes as feathers. Steele calls through

the wall of wings and her name is a gong. At dinnertime
her parents beg her from her room. She drifts down the hall, through

TV sounds and laundry. To them she is a cat. Her infinitesimal
smile, her hair a purple curtain. The pea soup scalds. Through

the window, she watches the moon, a skater on the sky's
frozen lake. She wills it to fall through.

II. What She Worries Forever Will Be

His fingers are squat sausages. He growls and sighs. Out
of sight, blessed by dark, her mouth perfects lies. Out-

side the sky is vacant. *Oh yes,* her mouth says. She knows he could
swallow her whole. When he says *love,* she shuts her eyes, out

for now of kindness and grit. She aches for curfew. She knows
he wants her kept and in white. She cringes when he cries out,

but he is gone in her glow. His promises are sharp-edged shells
she crumbles behind her back. He grinds out

mix tapes and cryptic notes, and she thinks, *Presto! Nothing.*
He is a factory of fear. His wants roar and rise. Out

of pity or malice, she feints into his waiting hands, her blankness
expert. Each night, she knows, he prays that he never finds out.

III. Where She'll Go Next

Maybe the desert. The sun's sure anger, the night's brittle cold, her
body quick and ready beneath the dust-drenched sky. There, she'll be bolder,

her voice like thunder—occasional and sure. She'll cull the bleached
bones of coyotes and string them like pearls. She'll unfold her

fingers to show cactus scars. Or maybe instead a strange city
of sirens and pigeons and tall, gloved men. There, she'll mold her

mouth into a lipsticked enigma. Bands will lace her name through songs.
She'll drink vodka, laugh broadly, her cigarettes hand-rolled. Or

she could go to Kenya, Fort Pierce, Juneau, Spain. She could fortune tell
or build homes, she could gamble, she could pan rivers for gold, her

hands plunged deep in riches. She imagines narrating her life
from an after-point. Now she is in a story no one ever told her.

LET'S LIVE IN THE BOOKS OF MY CHILDHOOD

"Presently they came to a freshly painted, white house overlooking the surf. It proved to be cool, clean, and inviting. Although it was late for luncheon, the woman in charge assured the girls she could serve them."

—Nancy Drew: *Mystery of the Tolling Bell*

Let's climb together up rickety stairways,
let's scramble through briars, let's dart
around carnival tents, the gypsies always
at our backs, the coarse-voiced caretaker
rounding the corner in his black sedan (yes,
don't panic, I know the tricks of escape),
let's speed off in your clanging jalopy, your hand
never on my knee, our pulses never slowing
to resting, and then drive me home under
an unspoiled sky (yes, we'll keep watch
for the jewel thief with the scar, don't worry,
I'll know him) and let *home* be decked in white
and cornflower blue, let it be oak and old lace,
let there be a narrow bed where I'll lie when I leave you
at the door, let the bed be cool when I slide in
(yes, I'll be fine, my father's here and crooks
turn in early), while you drive home
through the lamplit night, and then
come back the next day and let's do it again,
and yes, yes, I know there's the mystery to be solved,
but it always gets solved, and I wish you'd stop
missing the point, which is to live here, in this world

of sailboats and chums and exclamation points,
where luncheon is always served, where we'll never
vote or clean or fade, and we both know to tauten
our wrists when bound so we can twist free later,
and there, at the end, will be your jalopy again,
and a picnic at the seashore, maybe a palm reading,
maybe a boat race (never a wedding, never a death),
and the end will be no end but only a teaser
for the next summer-stung installment,
each plump blonde friend, each sallow-skinned man,
each telegram and flat tire and chloroformed rag
already in place, always, check, check, check.

READING *YM* AT THE POOL, AGE 12

Possibility glints in the lapis lanes
at her feet. When she gets home,
she will try the trick of lemons.
She will condition with mayonnaise.

She will practice holding her tongue
between her fingers so she won't gag
on the first kiss (sloppy and slipshod, she expects).
Long and rolled out before her, the summer

is a highway. She imagines stops
along the way: at Mile First-Mosquito-
Bite, pick up better posture. At Mile
Warm-Evening-at-Lickety-Split, pick up

The Confidence to Make Him Yours!
At Mile Three's-Company-Marathon,
pick up laughter that ripples like ribbon
in wind. She knows there is time

to fix the wrongs. She knows everything
is next: cool, dark theatres. Songs to roll
around in. Calls to sneak late at night, a towel
under the door so her crafted laugh

won't travel. She will learn new words
and then say them, their sharpness stinging
her tongue like the tart candies she eats all day.
The magazines will get none of it right.

In August, lightning will crack the backyard oak.
As the wound smokes, she will press
the hard bone just below her throat
but know that now there's no going back.

FOR THIS YOU HAVE NO REASON

In Sacramento, a Virgin Mary has begun spilling
blood from its stone eyes. Articles offer theories:

a prank, a rusting mineral. *There is no explanation*,
I say over and over, my heart tensed like a fist. Once,

at Chez la Mer, I watched a magician turn silver coins
into yellow fin tuna while diners oohed. When the room

shuddered with calls for the big reveal, I ducked
outside, humming to cover the sound of the secret.

Here are facts: the dog gone for a decade makes
its way to Arizona and finds its family still pining,

now joy-struck. The wooden Christ in St. Stephen's
Cathedral grows hair, and is groomed every year

before Easter. A friend's father saw three UFOs
zoom into a lit triangle, then shoot to far

corners of the lake-dark sky. He was not a man
who lied. For years I found playing cards facedown

on sidewalks, and each was the jack of hearts—
absurd, but I swear this is true. *Here*, each face said,

for this you have no reason. Each new finding shores up
something always close to collapse inside my ribs.

Let these strangenesses be like the impossible lizard's
tail: gone forever, because how could it be otherwise,

and then reappearing, iridescent and blood-warmed,
because how could it be otherwise?

HARE-LIP

"It is said that any pregnant woman who is startled by a hare or rabbit is likely to give birth to a child with a hare-lip."

—*Cassell's Dictionary of Superstitions*

First I stopped wine, gin, the sharp tang
of tequila. I stopped coffee. I stopped

swordfish. These were easy. Then I felt
slight movement inside me, light as a leaf,

and I stopped running, lest I jar something loose.
I stopped leaning forward against the sink

as I stroked on mascara. Then I stopped mascara,
so no poison could seep through my lashes.

One day I stumbled over a curb, and that evening
I burned my heeled boots. On my way

to the drugstore for vitamins, the car in front
of me skidded. I braked, swerved, lived,

and drove home. Then I stopped driving.
So many singers wailed *never* and *baby* and *bleed*

that I had to stop listening. I began humming
to fill the air, then felt how vibrations shook me

and learned silence. On my morning walk,
the horse in the field across the street stared,

and in its white blaze I saw death by lightning.
I stayed home after that. The yard seemed safe

until today, when the sun's new summer heat
muscled against my body. I imagined a great egg

poaching, so I went in and drew the curtains
for cool. I kept busy disconnecting appliances.

Then I sat still and tall in the center of my bed
until sundown. Now it's dusk, time of quiet

and colorless light. I'm careful. I crawl to the door,
inch out into the soft, blank air. But I hear the evening

grass rustle near me. Just in time I catch myself
from turning. I wrench my head upward, and see

instead the moon rising. There's nowhere left to look,
so I blink and blink until its twisted face is perfect.

SHE CONSIDERS TRADING HER SECRETS

These girls, she says. These girls, I could smite them.
These girls, if they knew about the tree inside me, or

the rabbit trap, or the plastic doll parts. If they knew
about the dog I walk each night in my dreams, her big

teeth showing, her paws like dinner plates. If they knew
how I like knowing she could eat me but chooses not to.

That is how I feel safest. These girls. If they saw me lit
by the dome light of my station wagon. If they saw me under

his hands during the ice storm. What would they say?
Would they kiss me? Would they share their licorice

and chlamydia? Would we talk about equations as if
they held the world? Oh, these girls. They are dumb

as bicycles. Their eyes like tree knots. Their smiles
like paper. If they knew that my world is not their world,

is gloaming-colored and damp, echoes with howls and bells,
floats in the space between the desert and the past—

would they ride the carousel next to me? Would they,
for once, give me the best horse?

DAILY

Some days you wake to the sound
of your own stomach whirring.
Some days the morning gray
feels like cotton in your mouth—
it's soft, and it suffocates.
Some days the sun flashes down
for ten minutes, or twenty, and in
those minutes you feel your veins
strong with blood and temerity,
you could laugh through
a tornado, you could hold a life
together with wire and spit
and be the pioneer you've always
known you were. Then the sun
fades out and you remember
how often the pioneers went mad.
This is how it goes, these days.
You blink on, then you blink
off. You think, what is the metaphor
for this? The wisteria is hinting
into bloom. The dropped pine limbs
have cracked the windshield.
The neighborhood creek is rushing
after rain—is it nature or poison?
You want to locate, locate, locate.
You want to hide, hide, hide.
And then you don't. You want

to sit on the roof of your house
with a six-pack of terrible beer
and rip off shingles one by one.
You want to go back to the boardwalk
amusements of your youth and ride,
again, the Gravitron, that hulking
spaceship that spun like a centrifuge.
That's the best you can do
for now. It's your life.
It is spinning, and you are in it.

The Sleeping Creature House

Tickets, please. Yes, we'll also accept scraps of paper
with your deepest fears scrawled on, and handshakes,
so long as they're quivery. Come in, come in.
Over here you'll see the sleeping lion. Yes, you may bury
your hands in his mane. We get that request a lot.
He's warm, isn't he? Asleep like that, he'll protect you.
Look at the two of you, like a sculpture titled "Equals."
Here is the sleeping American Staffordshire Terrier.
Admire his tree-trunk chest, his forelegs like rifles.
He'll never clamp his spring-trap jaw around your throat.
One click from you and he'd blitz through his paces.
We can tell. What an impressive master! This way, please.
Here is the death adder, imported from Australia. Sleeping,
he's misunderstood. Stroke his tiled scales, see his lovely
tongue flick toward breath. You must be a snake charmer!
Never have we seen him respond so sweetly. Finally,
the sleeping shark. See how she floats as she dozes.
See how defenseless she is, how fleshy, her gills so open.
You could dive in right now and nuzzle up to her rough skin.
The last case is empty. We're taking suggestions.
We're branching out. A hippopotamus. A crocodile.
Your memory of the long-toothed mailman. A scorpion.
Your terror of children, and of dying alone. Your guilt
from the Denver layover. An ocelot. Formidable
beasts, all. Tracking them is easy—we're professionals.
The hard part is beating them unconscious.

Before the Reunion (Her Lament)

Maybe if I'd hurled at least one brick
through a windshield. Maybe
if I'd jumped on the train
and clung, hobo-style, as it rocketed
over the river trestle. Maybe if
I hadn't quit gymnastics. If I'd lied
more. If I'd lied less. If I'd fallen
down the basement stairs
into the party. If I'd gotten
into the rumbling Datsun.
If I'd said *fuck off* instead of
I'm sorry. If I'd said *come over*
instead of *I hear something*.
If I'd looked at myself
in the mirror. If I'd stopped
ogling myself in the mirror.
If I'd smashed every mirror
and made talismans and disco balls
from the pieces.

THE GUIDANCE COUNSELOR TO THE GIRL

The test suggests an aptitude for solitary work.
Have you considered a career as a computer

programmer? Flower arranger? Planetarium
operator? No? What about zebrawood cultivation?

Minor-league mascotry? Those heads muffle
all voices, even your own. Column A indicates

a proclivity for nature. You may have more luck
as a bobcat than a sea turtle, a muskrat than a bobcat.

What do you mean, why? We just discussed
your inclination toward solitude! Here's the list

of promising careers. Muskrat we'll cross out.
Blue spruce on a half-acre? Nest-fleeing cardinal?

Maybe? Let's mark it. Throw-pillow by the fire?
Asphalt-dinged Route 40 road sign? Lost gold

stud in the sand? Anything? We'll keep going.
Abandoned Chevy in near-mint condition? One stone

in the Grand Canyon at sunset? No, I agree, too much
responsibility. How about this—the iron clapper

in a wind chime. Well, I don't know, my dear—
I imagine you'd have to create the wind yourself.

EVERYTHING AN AMULET OR OMEN

You scoff at the pinch of salt
over the shoulder, the tight inhale
before graveyards. These are amateur tricks.
You time your steps to tread on cracks

as carefully as crossing a trestle. You walk
under ladders, head up, eyes defiant.
You got yourself a black cat and named him
Lucky. Aren't you clever. Aren't you

your black cat's meow. You don't knock wood
or waste wishes on stars. No, you're a secret
agent, a specialist. Four taps on the door, four sips,
four nods, four yeses under cover of basement dark.

If you do it right, your brother's limbs
will stay intact. Timing is everything. If you
make it under the still-yellow light, A. won't
choke during dinner. If you make it into the drive

before the song ends, B. will not kill someone
while driving looped on Jäeger. Chance
is a shrewd fiend, but you, laser-focused,
can outwit it. Better not to look at clocks at all,

lest your eyes land on the age your father
will be when he dies young. Better not
to let the cat lick your skin, as the rough tongue
might mean a plane crash or house fire. A found

heads-up penny does nothing, as you know.
But a yellow leaf can protect. Like a red-suit
playing card, or a page from a book if it includes
the word *tomorrow*. Best to draw a dark line

through the word *disease* whenever
you read it. Best not to look at broken glass
or dying grass. Your head is humming. Let it.
It's the motor that will save you. Everyone.

LAMP

"It was once considered unlucky to go out at night without a lantern, as evil spirits could then...creep up on their human victims unobserved."

—Cassell's Dictionary of Superstitions

The mother, fingers fluttering like moths inside her robe pockets,
has urged caution. Again and again she's said it, flapping quietly.
The girl tosses her eyes upward. When the mother

looks out, all she sees is the closed hand of sky. They are
inside it. The mother thinks *gullet*. She thinks *chamber*.
She thinks of things that swallow and things that burst.

She wants to wrap the girl in neon, stud her skirt
with flash cubes. The mother thinks she sees, outside
the window, the white of an eye, the glint of a tooth.

She thinks she sees metal, the sea, a funnel cloud. But
she does not say this. She says only, *Pretty dark out*.
She breaks the word like a stick in two—*pret-ty*—

because this might make the girl laugh, and the laugh
might become a thread to tether them together.
But the girl's breath puffs out, once. Her large eyes close,

then open. It is as if she knows more than she does. *The dark
is nothing*, she says, her eyes locked upward again. *Yes*,
the mother says, and lets the great hand pluck the girl away.

3.

EMERGENCE

"Sixty-five years after an American P-38 fighter plane ran out of gas and crash-landed on a beach in Wales, the long-forgotten World War II relic has emerged from the surf and sand where it lay buried… [U]nusual weather caused the sand to shift and erode."

—AP article

The planet is warming toward a million revelations.
What next? The Nile, perhaps, will dry up, lift
its water veil on the aquatic circus that's spun

for centuries below the current: fire-eaters, jugglers,
a procession of pachyderms, revealed and stunned.
Mount Rushmore will collapse with wrecking ball drama,

and in place of the faces will be every lost pet,
all the vanished dogs and cats and pythons thriving
in a stone-sealed country of hydrants and mice. When

the South Pole slips away like an ice cube held
in a mouth, we'll find the world's largest emerald,
twice the size of Nebraska and greener than smog.

At the bottom of the Dead Sea, a simple aspen grove,
leaves rattling like coins in the new wind. And when
the warming air gently tongues away centuries of rock

and water, when the earth splits like a walnut to reveal
an ostrich, maybe we'll crack, too, let slip the parts
for which the world has no use: a high school girl's need

for a necklace of wriggling earwigs; a woman's deep
hunger for a handful of loam; a man's suffocating love
for bioluminescent squid (not to have one, but

to *be* one, to fly through starred darkness and light
his own way)—these longings so wrenching they are
nearly despair. There are things we keep chained,

because who would want to believe them? But here
at the end of the world, let the earth melt down.
Here at the end of the world, let us crumble open.

The '70s Aren't Coming Back

Never again will George bellow at Louise
on a school night. Never again will the audience
adore Florence. The soft plumes of Miss Maryland's
hair were sincere and fantastic, but ventriloquists
never won; Miss Texas would take it, if you knew
anything about beauty and you did. The couch
was velour and the color of bricks. Your mind
was a minefield—every wicked thought a tripwire
you sprung again and again until you evaporated
inside guilt's white blasts. The six o'clock news
hummed in the background like the cicadas outside
your window. What war? The couch was so soft.
Miss Maryland was a cockatiel. Your head
was a haunted factory, but there was cinnamon
in the spaghetti sauce. The O'Jays were on the radio.
You knew Rhoda Morgenstern and Spiro T. Agnew
and how to find the groove for "Brand New Key."
Sometimes you got trapped in dreams—waking
was a window you could see through but not open.
The studio audience wore red and beige; the host
had large, cheerful teeth. Door Number Three
revealed a horse, and the band played *wah-wah*,
but you wanted Door Number Three. No one
understood. You were locked in yourself all day,
all night, like the song that buzzed in your brain
when you were translucent with fever. Every movie

your parents watched ended with a sax solo. It floated
through the vents to where you almost slept.
You rode its waves straight into longing,
where you live now, where you'll live forever.

Dear Day,

Lately I am more aware of how easily
you might lope carelessly off into a fog
of never and gray, and so when you come
in the morning with your pincers on,
when you wake me with your snorts
and hacks, when you lie down next to me
with your scales poking all my soft places,
I hold you to me. The bruises will heal,
and it isn't your fault you're so spiny.
Day, you lower your monstrous head
and let me pat it. You are gleaming
and everything. You are genus unknown,
phylum unnamed. You glint and lumber,
you drool and growl. Soon, maybe,
you'll let me climb on your back. Soon,
maybe, we'll bullet together into forests
and glades and gladness. So stay. Walk
beside me with your armor on, breathe
flames at the beasts that bite. If I get singed,
it's okay. I'd pay levy upon levy
for your glittering shadow beside me.

SCALE

At the base of a mountain,
you are small, and the world
clicks smoothly over you.

At the base of a mountain,
you glow inside *almost*,
and few lights are so generous.

At the base of a mountain,
death is inevitable. Look
how the rock has swallowed
centuries. You could melt
into its sun-ovened roughness.

At the base of a mountain,
you see, in the hazeless light,
the revised version of yourself.
You think, I will do what it takes
to breathe this prickling air.
You think, I will turn alarm bells
into pine needles, and then
I'll walk over them. You think,
I'll let my hair grow again.
I'll eat apples, avocados.

You think, there is nothing
ahead and nothing behind.
You think of a thousand songs
and choose silence. It whistles
softly to you. No. It's whistling
to the mountain. It doesn't
even know you're there.

POSTCARDS FROM HER ALTERNATE LIVES

1.
Each day the city unhinges its jaw and I climb inside.
I sing show tunes and polish its teeth. At night, I ride
its lit scales into glittered, show-stopping dreams.

2.
Sister, the desert is more even than I dreamed. On each
rock rests a bowl of water, a wooden flute, a lizard.
The clouds swoop into the shape of my fears, then
blow off into the next county.

3.
I live between mountains and take my smallness,
like a pill, on waking. Always I'll be only one
more moving part, blurred in snow and stone.
I'll never fall for the slick con of consequence.

4.
Bright, or secret, or ghosted, towns fall into place
like the corner pieces of a jigsaw puzzle. All the sky
pieces look the same. I can't fit the fragments
of clouds together.

5.
This place is as I never left it: the neon sub shop
on the corner, the junior high. My house is an aquarium
filled with tulips. My mouth is a tulip filled with dust.

A Short Biography of the American People by City

In Surprise, every day is a party, streamers
in the trees and piñatas bursting. No one from Surprise

visits Dismal, though they've heard of its fog-
shrouded hills and barren stream beds. In Dismal they dream

of Happy and What Cheer, but it's all they can do
to someday make it to Boring, where homes are narrow

but clean and each dog is part Lab, part spaniel. The boys
in Boring long for the girls of Peculiar—they've heard

tales of leather and feathers, of lipstick the color
of tin cans and long hair the shade of the sky. The girls

of Peculiar are sick of the men from Ogle driving out
"just to visit." The girls are no fools. A camp counselor

once told them in hushed tones about her road trip
from Blueball to Intercourse to Climax, and since then

the girls have been wiser. Mothers want to pack them off
to Okay, where everyone's shoes are polished and all

boys under eighteen have cowlicks. When things go wrong
in Okay—the mayor's affair, the schoolteacher's lustiness—

the offenders start over in Nameless. The tired find strength
in Hot Coffee. The spiraling in Parachute. The hungry head

to Lame Deer, the clever to Riddle. A few men sneak off
in the night for Flasher and Footville, heads ducked

but thrilled to be fleeing Embarrass. And sooner or later,
when all their homes prove poorly named—when streamers

drop from trees, when cowlicks flatten, when poodles
start populating the parks—they all migrate east, crossing

rivers and hills to find one another in Fear Not.

Desire: Three Girls

I. Mississippi, 1958

In the violet evening the radio crackles
like a candy wrapper. You hate Eisenhower
for interrupting *The Cisco Kid*. Mama hides
everything in her angry bouffant. You think
she is beautiful—mouth a coral slash, lashes
like spider legs. You tell her she is Miss
America and she turns away. Your father left
for town in '54 and hasn't brought the ham
home yet. Most nights you sup on the glances
of bicycling boys. The air is wet and bright.
You might call it *languid*. You in high summer
are languid, your limbs too stick-like still
to cozen longing, though you know that ache
like you know the translucent lizards on the stuck
screen door. You have a moss-drenched oak
and a tire swing. When you spin high, your bare
legs flash against leaves. No one scolds you.
Every house on the street has eyes. In a glass jar
you corral an army of fireflies. When you
release them, they blind the houses. You know
because when you leave no one's watching.

II. Pennsylvania, 1961

All summer you've practiced your Jayne Mansfield
stretch beside Becca's leaf-clogged pool. Pottstown
in August is an egg sizzling on the black skillet

of Pennsylvania. You dream of New England, where
you've never been, where Mr. Smithson will take you
and buy you town homes and brooches, where streets

are strung with white lights and summer is women
in moss-colored shifts and golden, minted drinks. Your Coke
is an injustice, and Mr. Smithson understands. His daughter

can't handle bourbon, but you're a siren. Back outside,
you dive into the shallow end and swan up just in time.
No one knows how close you came. No one ever will.

III. Maryland, 1964

The rental cottage gives you the creeps,
its corners dark and peopled with blank-
eyed dolls. But outside the sun is an open
mouth, calling. You hold your breath
and sink into the sea, hoping the red-suited
guard will save you. When you pop up,
a bright cork, he's dozing. All afternoon
you loll in the sand; its billion tiny mouths
leave bites on your palms and thighs.
On the boardwalk, you drip vinegar
on fries and gauge your lips' pinkness
by the sting. Pickup trucks drive by,
all whoop and holler. The catcalls
are aloe on your skin. One truck pulls over.
Your name and age ripple out in a ribbon
of lies. Suddenly your hair is a triumph
of salt and shine. You are ablaze, the cottage
too airless ever to hold you. In the rusted
truck bed, a keg, a blanket. You glance up.
The sun's open mouth says: Go.

The Books Fill Her Apartment Like Birds

First just a few, then more, then more—
this one a gift, this one a pity adoption. They flutter
as she passes. They call
when she comes home. She strokes them,
soothes them. They flap, agitated.

She tries to nap, but their cries
are constant. They are starving.
They will not be placated. She says to her friends,
Look how they need me! She wraps herself
in their chattering demands.

They perch on her chest, her hands. Her bones
begin to decorate her skin. She eats
nothing now but what they feed her,
seed by seed. She thinks, *Now I am
beginning to exist.* Only at night

does she sometimes wish they'd quiet down.
Through the wall of sleep, she hears their shrieks
like pinpricks of light. In dreams, black lines of letters
drift into bars. She wakes
with her hands clenched like claws.

A Catalogue of My Wants from Age 16 to the Present

The early part:

        For my street to dead-end in a ghost town.
        To read every word I couldn't
        pronounce. To curve elegantly under
        the pressure of a tongue like a question mark,
        like a lady. To disappear. To own
        a flying car. Or at least have a flying dream.
        Anything to get off the fucking ground.

Later:

        For my insides to match the rocking quiet.
        Or for the river to burst into flame.
        To walk by the sleeping houses all night
        without needing to sleep myself. To
        want to ride the train over the trestle,
        clinging, whooping. To be enviably
        twirling, enviably grave. To cause
        each set of eyes to anchor on me.

Later still:

        To live inside a roiling sun. To see the sky
        emptying of love letters and toffees instead
        of rain. To strap myself to myself until
        I had learned a valuable lesson. To collapse
        with all drama and no ego. To find any perfect
        mouth. To climb the ladder of my ribcage

until I reached my own brain, and to fall
asleep there, exhausted. To issue decrees
from the miasma of gin and wonder.

Now:

For my street to dead-end in a ghost town.
For my insides to match the rocking quiet.
To read love letters until I learn
a valuable lesson. To curve elegantly
under wonder. To ride gin and flames.
To issue decrees to myself. To collapse
my own brain. To disappear, whooping.
To fall asleep, enviably twirling. To be
a flying dream. To live inside every word.

How It Ends: Three Cities

#1: Austin, Texas

This morning we woke to the grackles. Their mouths open, tails oil-black against the blacker pavement. Some had closed their eyes; others had died staring. Cars stopped on Congress and were left, hunched like boulders. The elms, always bright with cries, were still. We didn't call work, just sleepwalked to the Red Pony Lounge and dropped into silence. Now someone puts Sam Cooke on the jukebox, "Cupid," and I think of the girl with the gun. The man across from me reaches into his coat pocket and pulls out a bird. Everyone shrieks, draws back, hisses about disease. I touch its small head. Its eyes are closed. I want it to wake up. To see what's left, even if it's only this bar, this green drink rimmed with glowing salt, this long-gone song caught up in smoke like light.

#2: New York, New York

By lunchtime, the city is swathed in sweetness. A woman says Bit-O-Honey. Her son says roasted almonds. Old men find one another to talk of fifth grade snow days. On Ludlow, a young man veers from a funeral motorcade in search of lemon meringue. A paralytic woman rises, walks to the freezer, scoops mouthful after mouthful of Rocky Road. In Central Park, a man takes a bottle from his backpack. He builds a perfect snowman and bathes it tenderly in maple syrup. He leans in to kiss it. A feuding couple falls silent in front of a window display of petit fours, chocolate tortes, marzipan apricots. After eating, they brush sugar gently from one another's mouths. A middle school teacher opens the window and students stream from it, called by the air, drifting skyward on the aroma of vanilla extract, as clear and sharp as winter.

#3: Okemah, Oklahoma

At first the animals don't seem strange. Most twilights the town is full of stray
dogs, alley cats. But the hamster? The iguana? Only when she sees the guinea
pig emerge from the garden soil, shake itself off, and trundle down the
sidewalk, does she begin to understand. Across the way the one-eyed tabby
bursts from beneath the oak. Goldfish leap down the street's puddles. Hermit
crabs scuttle over lawns, and cockatiels preen dirt from their wings. She hears
a sound from the movies, and turns to see Major Luther's old appaloosa
galloping down Birch Street. It seems wrong, she thinks, for them to come back
only to vanish again. But then Preacher Man, her golden retriever, dives into
her lap, and as the stars go black she is laughing.

WITHOUT CEREMONY

Once, many skies ago, we drove across the ache
of Kansas straight to the base of a large mountain.
We were nearly engaged. We were close to knowing
each other. At the peak I couldn't breathe and I
was elated. A fear with a name and I named it. Hypoxia.
Asphyxia. Things we might call a daughter. Later,
we played on pinball machines from the '30s.

There was a natural soda spring. I still can't explain it.
Something else I loved. There were animals
that popped from the mountainsides, built of curled horns
and indifference. Our raft nearly wrapped
around a boulder. At the take-out point, I jumped in
and almost drowned from the weight of water
ballooning my jacket. I didn't drown. Neither

did you. I loved that, too. I learned that gin
comes from the juniper tree. Could we name
a daughter Juniper? There was an early evening the color
of whiskey, all the trees sending out their air
of clean and quiet, six hummingbirds spinning
their wings around us on our cabin porch. On a hike
too hard, lightning flashed. The ground growled.

Here, too, I thought we might die. Then we didn't.
That night the primavera had just been invented.
We were toasting syrah to luck and odds. Outside,
the night dropped its blanket of lake water.
But inside a fire burned. It was meant to be
rustic. It succeeded, or we let it. Something
always worried me, my fear a constant shark,

but there it stopped circling, grew feathers.
It nested in the rafters, suddenly a quiet starling.
One night we ate chili rellenos. One night we drove
far out. We were lost in a strange neighborhood.
Meteors blitzed over the dome of sky without ceremony.
You held my head in your hands. We stood there.
We stood and heard lowing. We stood and heard wind.

SOMEWHERE IN THE HEAP OF MINUTES

there is a ride called the Zipper—red, blue,
yellow-painted, girls shrieking from the upside-

down cages, the grass below lit and littered.
There is a summer evening scored by the hiss

and buzz of the mosquito zapper. There is
a bowl of mojitos in a crowded kitchen,

the first taste of mint and lime and fizz
shaming the limp muscles of sorrow.

There is a sparrow falling and arcing up
and falling again into a gold-tinged yard.

There is a gold-hinged locket
in an unlocked box; inside, a photograph

of the future. There is a bright morning
when the cold is a lockbox, and icicles spike

the eaves like shining weapons. There is the ease
with which one smoke-blued twilight becomes night

becomes morning. There is the highlight
and lowlight on the lake, the inlet, the sound

at sunset. There is the sound at sunset
of neighborhood beagles crying down the distance,

and the knowledge that this is what will remain.
Sometimes the minutes add up to an old song

and radio crackle. Sometimes they add up
to that movie, you know the one, with the kids lost

in the woods and the good ending. Sometimes
they add up to spinning and shrieks and the girls

on the Zipper. Always they add up to a plea for more,
a hand closing around nothing, then opening again.

Also Available from saturnalia books:

Ladies & Gentlemen by Michael Robins

Xing by Debora Kuan

Other Romes by Derek Mong

Faulkner's Rosary by Sarah Vap

Gurlesque: the new grrly, grotesque, burlesque poetics
edited by Lara Glenum and Arielle Greenberg

Tsim Tsum by Sabrina Orah Mark

Hush Sessions by Kristi Maxwell

Days of Unwilling by Cal Bedient

Letters to Poets: Conversations about Poetics, Politics, and Community
edited by Jennifer Firestone and Dana Teen Lomax

My Scarlet Ways by Tanya Larkin
Winner of the Saturnalia Books Poetry Prize 2011

The Little Office of the Immaculate Conception by Martha Silano
Winner of the Saturnalia Books Poetry Prize 2010

Personification by Margaret Ronda
Winner of the Saturnalia Books Poetry Prize 2009

To the Bone by Sebastian Agudelo
Winner of the Saturnalia Books Poetry Prize 2008

Famous Last Words by Catherine Pierce
Winner of the Saturnalia Books Poetry Prize 2007

Dummy Fire by Sarah Vap
Winner of the Saturnalia Books Poetry Prize 2006

Correspondence by Kathleen Graber
Winner of the Saturnalia Books Poetry Prize 2005

The Babies by Sabrina Orah Mark
Winner of the Saturnalia Books Poetry Prize 2004

Velleity's Shade by Star Black / Artwork by Bill Knott

Polytheogamy by Timothy Liu / Artwork by Greg Drasler

Midnights by Jane Miller / Artwork by Beverly Pepper

Stigmata Errata Etcetera by Bill Knott / Artwork by Star Black

Ing Grish by John Yau / Artwork by Thomas Nozkowski

Blackboards by Tomaz Salamun / Artwork by Metka Krasovec

The Girls of Peculiar was printed using the font Gil Sans.

www.saturnaliabooks.org